DIVORCED

AND CHRISTIAN

DIVORCED
AND CHRISTIAN

Alice Stolper Peppler

Publishing House
St. Louis   London

Concordia Publishing House, St. Louis, Missouri
Concordia Publishing House Ltd., London, E. C. 1
Copyright © 1974 Concordia Publishing House
Manufactured in the United States of America

Library of Congress Cataloging in Publication Data

Peppler, Alice Stolper.
    Divorced — and Christian.

    1. Divorce. I. Title.
BT707.P46   248'.84   74-4505
ISBN 0-570-03189-3

To

ASLAN THE LION*

who appeared again and again,

warmed me with his breath,

and blessed me with new life.

* *ASLAN* is Christ
in C. S. Lewis's
"Narnia" allegories

Contents

Foreword	11
1. Introduction to Divorce	13
2. Shock, Despair	16
3. Physical Reactions	21
4. Pastor's Help	25
5. Telling the News	29
6. Family Help	33
7. Children	37
8. Means of Coping	44
9. Ex-Mate	49
10. Dating	54
11. Extreme Doubt, Faith Challenged	61
12. Recovery from Doubt, Faith Rebuilt	69
13. Ready to Begin Anew	75
14. New Life — and Love	83
Postscript	91

Foreword

This book deals with Christian divorce — not the causes, not the church's position, not the "rightness" or "wrongness" of the parties involved, not anything but the effects. It offers no recipes for patching up marriages and proffers no hope for same. It is for people who have already gone through all these steps. It is for people who have tried to save their marriages and failed. It is for people who must now live with the failure. It is for people who once loved, and perhaps still do. It is for people who feel the pain of the slash as the marriage bonds are severed.

The divorced who grieve, grieve doubly — first because of their loss, and second because of the world's attitude over against their state and their sorrow. At a time when they need comfort and understanding most, they may be getting it least. It is assumed they had control over their affairs and as such have no cause now for grief. The poor, the sick, the widowed — all are "justified" in their lamenting. Not so the divorced. And so a book for them and their own special sorrow.

Scattered throughout this volume is free verse that should help you share more fully the experience of divorce and begin to understand how it actually feels. I wrote the poems at the time of my separation and divorce, and I found them a means of coping that had a great healing effect. They touch the heart of my experience.

Portions of the Psalms begin and end each chapter of this book. Along with the book of Job, the Psalms have been very meaningful to me since living through a crisis.

It was through the rereading of specific Psalms and free verse that I could "relive" the experience to record its effects.

It is healthy to forget the trauma of divorce, to lock it away in the cellar of one's subconscious, and to live instead in the present and future. But periodically our Lord calls us to minister to others whose "now" is our past. Fulfilling this call means reliving personal pain, but only as the healed help the hurt can love reign. It is worth the sharing if readers who are living the grief can be comforted in learning that what they are experiencing is very natural and, thanks to God, only temporary.

O Lord, my God, I cried unto Thee,
　　and Thou hast healed me.
O Lord, Thou hast brought up my soul
　　from the grave;
Thou hast kept me alive,
　　that I should not go down to the pit.
Sing unto the Lord, O ye saints of His,
　　and give thanks at the remembrance
　　of His holiness.
For His anger endureth but a moment;
　　in His favor is life:
Weeping may endure for a night,
　　but joy cometh in the morning.
　　Psalm 30:2-5 KJV

1 * Introduction to Divorce

How amiable are Thy tabernacles,
O Lord of hosts!
My soul longeth, yea, even fainteth
for the courts of the Lord;
My heart and my flesh crieth out
for the living God.
Psalm 84:1-2 KJV

It's all over. One final session in court and a life together is over. If the marriage had ended in death (you muse), there would have been a funeral. Your friends would have been with your mate or you for the final service. Word and Sacrament would have been a comfort. Next Sunday there would have been prayers for the survivors. The grief could have been open, and even proud. One need not apologize for death.

But this is divorce . . . and divorce is completely and utterly without honor. The church has no prayers for the divorced. No congregational voice will rise up to heaven on behalf of your loss.

And now you are alone. No matter who is with you, you are alone. You have begun a life that is totally unlike anything you have ever lived. It is not merely going back to the single state; it is to a new state that you're going. You have left your settled, comfortable, married world and entered an unsettled, separate one — a "limbo" you'll never completely share or explain to your single, married, or

13

widowed friends. You'll soon learn what all divorced know —
that there is no way to "tell it like it is" to outsiders —
that there is no vicarious experience for divorce.

You've never had any preparation for this new state . . .
not really. You remember asking what it's like to be a father,
a mother, a husband, a wife. You remember querying occupa-
tions. You remember a whole childhood of multidimensional
training, but unless it was a reality in your home, you never
asked what it's like to be divorced, and no one ever considered
preparing you for it. It would have been negative and self-
defeating, perhaps, to even admit its possibility. But now
its reality is even more negative. And you're not prepared . . .
not really. And your family and friends aren't prepared . . .
not really.

It's eerie. It's unreal. All time has stopped. You thought
hard labor had begun with that first contraction so long ago.
You timed and considered every contraction over the
months or years. You hoped the divorce would have been
final — the delivery room. But there's no relief yet. You're
still back at the hospital door. You've only begun. And it
will not be an easy delivery.

You're all alone,
     but not really.
The Spirit . . . the Son . . . the Father . . .
     they're all there, too.
Really!

God is our Refuge and Strength,
     a very present help in trouble.
Therefore will not we fear,
     though the earth be removed,

*and though the mountains
be carried into the midst of the sea;
though the waters thereof
roar and be troubled
though the mountains shake
with the swelling thereof.*
Psalm 46:1-3 KJV

2 * Shock, Despair

Unto thee will I cry, O Lord, my Rock;
be not silent to me: lest if Thou be
silent to me, I become like them that
go down into the pit.

      Psalm 28:1 KJV

For my days are consumed like smoke,
and my bones are burned as a hearth.
My heart is smitten, and withered like grass;
so that I forget to eat my bread.
By reason of the voice of my groaning
my bones cleave to my skin.
I am like a pelican of the wilderness:
I am like an owl of the desert.
I watch, and am as a sparrow alone
upon the housetop.

      Psalm 102:3-7 KJV

The shock of the marriage death occurs long before the divorce decree. When you first suspected your marriage was ending you wondered what was happening to you. You didn't feel joyous or tragic or free or despairing — you just didn't feel! You were in a twilight zone of shock and unreality — a nightmarish suspension from which you vaguely expected to awaken. You were a stranger to yourself; your mate was still more an unknown; and nothing made sense. You cried for help as if from outer space, with no one "real" around to hear.

HELP!

Help

h
e
l
p

if
only

Senselessness may have hovered for some time, but eventually it gave way to a feeling of loss. There is grief in marriage-breaking. It is natural enough when one still loves, but it exists even when one doesn't. A union, however bad it is, cannot be dissolved without a feeling of loss.

If the loss is especially dear or too overpowering, you may react with despondency. Strength sapped and spirit crushed by the demon of despair, you will be conscious of evil forces all around you. They'll be grinning, these grim phantoms, just waiting for you to give up so they can begin their victory feast. You will know too well the psalmist's anguished cry from the depths of nothingness, from the pits of hopelessness. You will think of, and perhaps seriously consider, suicide. You will wish to escape . . . to escape . . . to escape . . . but it will seem impossible.

Nowhere
is too
low.

Swirling . . .
darker and deeper . . .

Darkness
everywhere

Brimful living goblet
of doom and horror

They drink and rejoice,
and I

hate myself . . .

Peter walks on the water
above the mud,
but not alone,
never alone . . .
impossible.

Nowhere
is too
low.

Even there
Thou art there

You're in mud — the muddy mire of despair. If you were raised in the church, you may recall your childhood Christian training — the memorization of Bible passages and hymns, the warnings of Satan as the roaring lion, the assurance of God's love and comfort, the innocent firm trust of your confirmation day, the zeal of your European forefathers tolling their faith in a new world.

Thoughts flash through your mind, but before they are completed, new observations appear. Everything runs together. Your brain hops from this to that. You can't concentrate. You can't get organized. You flounder. You debate with yourself. You understand only one thing — your confusion.

God is LO
VE and of course you have Christi
an upbringing and so
hate, horror, LO (?loco?) VE
encompasses all.
ComeuntoMeandIwillgiveyourest.
Memmmmmory   work
to withstand the RoaRRRRing li
on.

Once in confirmation
"be thou faithful unto death"
the endless rote — rote — rote
the church bells
in the forest from Franken-
muth . . .

where is that Faith?
crushhh
ed in con (founding, fusing
flicting) Chicago? fool(ish) and fu
tile. lame Luther
an, lamenting . . . lost . . .
GOD IS
(I have loved thee with an everlasting) LOVE
waitontheLord

WAIT

on the Lord

Again and again you will tell yourself that God is with
you. And again and again you will wonder. Back and forth,
over and over, you'll thrash about in this net you find yourself in. You will question almost everything you ever
learned — truth, honor, friends, church, and the faith of your

19

fathers, But you will not discount the reality of God's love. It is still too soon to give in to doubt. You will tell Job's advisers who sneer in the back of your mind to desist. The world can be questioned, but not yet God. You thrash . . . but you still hold onto the line. . . .

Out of the depths have I cried
unto Thee, O Lord.
Lord, hear my voice:
Let thine ears be attentive
to the voice of my supplications.

If Thou, Lord, shouldest mark iniquities,
O Lord, who shall stand?
But there is forgiveness with Thee,
that Thou mayest be feared.
I wait for the Lord, my soul doth wait,
and in His Word do I hope.
Psalm 130:1-5 KJV

3 * Physical Reactions

Save me, O God; for the waters are
come in unto my soul.
I sink in deep mire, where there
is no standing:
I am come into deep waters, where
the floods overflow me.
I am weary of my crying;
my throat is dried; mine eyes
fail while I wait for my God.
Psalm 69:1-3 KJV

There will have been tears before the divorce —
there will be tears after. And they may make no sense.
They may be contradictory — first for this, then for just the
opposite. They may not be logical, but they will be real.

Even after the initial shock has passed, you will be
disturbed. For all your outward appearance, you will be
anything but calm and stable. There may be times when you
sit at a desk, stand at a stove, ride on a bus, and literally
shake all over. You may lose part of your hearing or even
faint periodically — with no past history or no physical
cause. Or perhaps hysteria may become an old friend.

You may develop headaches, or stomachaches, or trem-
bling hands, or loss of memory. You may become over-
active for a period and then listless for another. You may
fumble along at work or sit mindlessly daydreaming at home.
You can think of nothing. You can react to nothing.

Nothing comes
and settles
    and sits
    and sits
Her bags are packed
with mere nil
    so heavy
    so dead
in every room
She is sitting
    just sitting

You may begin eating too much — you may have no appetite for food. You may have insomnia night after night — you may seek sleep as an escape.

sink
    into sleep

the wonderful escape

head dizzy from drink
mind numbing, gratefully

SLEEP!
    Great Sleep
i welcome you

be mine for now
you're all i have.

You are bewildered; you cannot keep from musing again and again regarding the cause of your condition. Your reflections are exasperating, and you try unsuccessfully to stabilize your reactions. You look for logical explanations, for rationalizations, for ego-protective arguments, for answers . . . .

22

You wish you had professional help; you definitely do not want professional help. You desire to talk to someone and bare your soul; you refuse to talk to anyone and bare your soul. You yearn for the intelligence and insight to comprehend and act; you crave the simplicity and insensitivity to be unaware and passive.

And sometimes you digress —

When I was young,
a toddler still,
I had a dream
beyond my will.

And in the darkness
to my dread,
I saw a porcupine
beside my bed.

Night after night
he was there,
my dreadful symbol,
my thing of fear.

I miss that porcupine
beside my bed,
his quills seem harmless,
peaceful his head.

The beast is replaced
by pressure and strife,
the conflicts and pain,
the frustrations of life.

Instead of this horror,
oh that I could will,
beside me now
a porcupine still!

You drift off to sleep, childhood prayers on your lips . . . .

Commit thy way unto the Lord;
Trust also in Him;
And He shall bring it to pass.
      Psalm 37:5 KJV

4 * Pastor's Help

Blessed is he whose transgression
is forgiven,
whose sin is covered.
Blessed is the man unto whom
the Lord imputeth not iniquity,
and in whose spirit
there is no guile.
Psalm 32:1-2 KJV

For years you've attended church and seen your pastor at work. He's baptized, communed, preached, taught, confirmed, buried, and who knows what else. You've liked him very much for this, a little for that, and perhaps not at all for something else. You think you know your pastor fairly well . . . perhaps you do. But you will get to know him better — much better.

For probably the first time in your life, you are desperately in need of a counselor. Spiritual, emotional, practical counseling — this is what you must have! You look around and see who's available, who could possibly help. No matter what assistance is forthcoming from family and friends, there is a special need that can only be filled by a pastor.

You feel that for you, not just any minister will do. You'll need to expose your soul, your very being. You'll need to scrutinize your life, your feelings, your actions.

25

You'll need to confess your sins. You'll need to hear God's forgiveness. You'll need to be assured of it . . . .

And so you want a minister who will be exceptionally loving and understanding — one who you feel will not be shocked or sit in judgment. Hopefully, you can turn to your very own pastor. Now you will really get to know him — and he, you. If told in time, he will help you try to save your marriage; if not, he will help you adjust to its failure. He will let you talk, and will talk to you, more frankly than you've ever experienced. He will advise you, encourage you, pray with and for you, and in such ways "love" you in witness of God's love.

But remember, he also will fail you. There will be times when he won't have the time or the ability or the patience to cope with one or another of your problems. He has no divine nature as our Lord — only a human nature. For all his love, your difficulties will not be the only ones in his concern. He will fail you — count on it! You can no more expect perfection of him than you do of yourself or anyone else.

Be grateful instead for all he does give you! He is evidence of the Spirit of God. Accept what he gives. You will remember his contribution for the remainder of your life. You will remember him as the personification of God's love.

Some ministers are
BLOOD AND THUNDER.
Flamboyantly fuming
the flambeau
of ferocity,

they assert God
at the expense of man.

Some ministers are
MASSIVE MILLSTONES

looping the letter of the Law,
until their aphorisms
asphyxiate.

but my minister
is just a man . . .
when he mounts
the pedestal
to preach,
he is still
on the
ground.
and when he holds out
his hand to heal,
the cripple
comforts

just a man . . .
who will pray
in your pathological
pit
and descend
into your
depths
of dearth.
embracing your pain,
searing your scar,
he is a handbook
to hope

just a man . . .
innately intense
and wise to the world,

he sees sin
in cyclorama,
and with sagacious simplicity
grasps the Gospel
and lives
Love

---

*The steadfast love of the Lord
is from everlasting to everlasting.*
Psalm 103:17 RSV

5 * Telling the News

Lord, I cry unto Thee;
make haste unto me;
Give ear unto my voice,
when I cry unto Thee.
Let my prayer be set forth
before Thee as incense,
And the lifting up of my hands
as the evening sacrifice.
Psalm 141:1-2 KJV

Only your very best friends know of your separation . . . and you didn't tell them until you had to . . . . The neighbors have started to wonder where your mate is; it won't be long before everyone suspects. Yesterday you received a wedding invitation addressed to "Mr. and Mrs." It is bad enough to be reminded of weddings — how are you going to gather the courage to respond to an invitation for the two of you?

You keep answering phone calls for your mate. How long will you be able to think up excuses for the absence? And what do you say to old acquaintances who unknowingly ask about your husband or wife? There's no proper or satisfying way to tell the truth. If you try to be light and casual, you may appear callous and unfeeling. If you reveal inner fears and frustrations, you may appear unbalanced or bitter.

Your friends are in the same awkward position. How do they respond to the news? There is no "right way" for them either. If they have run into your spouse, should they tell you or should they feign ignorance? In what way should they become involved? Should they take sides? Can they become involved without taking sides? They are unsure. They do not know how to behave. They do not know what is expected of them from you . . . from your mate . . . .

But their uncertainty is nothing compared to yours. You dread confrontations with people. You even dread attending church. You desperately need the assurance of God's love, but you desperately need to escape the questioning words or looks of members. You're sure some couples feel superior to you because they have stayed together for the better *and* the worse. You would just as soon avoid them. You know others will show only love, acceptance, and sympathy, but you'd just as soon avoid them too for now. Even sympathy can hurt — it points up your need so vividly.

You realize you'll have to take hold of yourself and start some plan of action. For one thing, you must admit that you're separated. You begin, for example, to start signing greeting cards with only your name, and sometimes you pen a brief note of explanation. You encourage those who know of the divorce to tell others so you can avoid the embarrassment.

You begin correcting yourself when you refer to "we" instead of "I" in conversations. This is not easy, for years of habit do not soon reverse, and it's difficult to rephrase what is natural. You are not widowed, however, and references to the ex-mate will more likely evoke curiosity or disapproval than matter-of-factness or understanding. So you try . . . you try to change your speech. Yet day after day you find yourself slipping into the old patterns.

Faith in your marriage gone, your attitude towards

other people's is also changing. You are slightly envious over what they have, but also slightly suspect. You wonder if, put to the test, their marriages would endure.

simple —
unlittered —
unhampered —
unreal.
happiness with icing . . .
don't ask for cake,
it may exist.

You start noticing flaws in friends' marriages. Now and then the partners point them out to you; perhaps they think the admission will be comforting. Some muse how lucky you are; oh, if only they had their independence! They complain about this or that lack in their mates and even look to you for sympathy. They confide in you, yet they don't know quite how to take you now that you are "available." You are to be pitied . . . on the other hand, you could develop into a threat.

You reflect on your own marriage disaster. You reflect on the sandpits in others' marriages. You begin to think of the world of the married as the world of the superficial — a mere facade of happiness. You've taken off your wedding band, and it's as if you stepped outside and are looking into the window of a 19th-century institution.

You begin to doubt if you could ever love again. The married around you don't seem truly happy; maybe there is no such state. Perhaps you have been desiring the wrong thing. Perhaps the only way to achieve peace and happiness is to let nothing get through to you . . . to let nothing move you.

I have observed the statues,
self-composed and silent . . .

and I envy their fixed smiles.
I am jealous of their hard strength
and their unbending essence.
The statues are lasting,
their emotion unchanged.
They are calm, content, and cold . . . .

Someday I will be as you,
        marble throughout . . .
And they will look
        and pass on . . .
And though one pauses to touch,
        I will be untouched.
Though they move me,
        I will remain unmoved.
And if they melt me and recast,
        I will mold the mold.
Strong as steel,
        hard as diamond,
                fixed as eternity.
I will observe these plastics with pity.

You are a doubter.

You know God loves . . .

But few are like God . . . .

Create in me a clean heart, O God,
and renew a right spirit within me.
Cast me not away from Thy presence,
and take not Thy Holy Spirit from me.
Restore unto me the joy of Thy salvation,
and uphold me with Thy free Spirit.
Psalm 51:10-12 KJV

6 * *Family Help*

Make haste, O God, to deliver me;
  make haste to help me, O Lord. . . .
I am poor and needy;
  make haste unto me, O God.
Thou art my Help and my Deliverer;
  O Lord, make no tarrying.
  Psalm 70:1, 5 KJV

For all the times you wanted independence from your parents or siblings in the past, you need them now. If they live nearby, you consult with them often. You tell them your problems so often they know the words by memory. And even if they don't really know how to help, they try, and that's all you ask. You appreciate them as you never have before.

You, my sister
  lately appreciated
  dearly, dearly loved
Because you are you
  I am blessed.

If your family lives elsewhere, you beg them to come and stay for a time. Phone calls, letters, short visits all help, but you meet each new day with fear you won't make it through. In the darkest of night you call out for your mother, just as you did when you needed her as a child. And you are comforted, just remembering . . . .

33

mother

in all the world
the one who feels

    exactly . . .

especially in sorrow,
    and in need of solace,
i call to you . . .
you
    my mother

in times as this
    you come to me.
in times as this
    no one is closer.
lightly
    i feel your touch of love.
softly
    i hear your words of comfort
completely
    i experience you.
you . . .
    all that is you . . .
and for that moment
    i need no more . . .

mother

in all the world
the one who feels
    exactly . . .

Depressed and discouraged, you may not be able to camouflage your condition from your children. Once in a while even your youngest may literally embrace and comfort you when you lose emotional control. Then again, just recalling the strength and loving spirit of a Christian parent will abate your loneliness. You'll feel refreshed and vow to allow nothing to ever take that gift away from you.

Unless you are a statistical exception, your ex-mate's family seems to have forgotten you. You mourn the loss of those you loved. You yearn for their understanding . . . even when it's not possible.

During the long days and nights you cannot forget your divorce. You are so lonely. You are so separated. You are so cut off. . . .

I am so lonely tonight —
                so alone —
        walking aimlessly,
        wanting to talk, to share, to love . . . .

The baby cries into the night
        asking for consolation — easy to give.

Nothing consoles me,
        no tranquillizer eases the lifeless
        numbing of the spine,
        the sick deadness within . . .
        no, not the book half finished,
        the endless cigarette ashes,
        the wine barely sipped,
Nothing dulls the active mind.

Oh, for a friend now,
        someone to listen to laugh,
        to comfort — to cry!
I stand by empty.
        "until death do us part"

I am so lonely tonight —
                so alone —

Whatever loneliness means to the child or the single person, it means something quite different to you. Your marriage has been torn apart. You remember it as a whole union; now it is an amputee. There exists a loneliness of incompleteness that only the formerly married realize. You tell God about it night after night. You figure He knows what it's like, but you tell Him anyway, just to make sure. You cast your care upon Him, for you know He cares for you.

To Thee I lift up my eyes,
O Thou who art enthroned
in the heavens!
Psalm 123:1 RSV

7 * Children

Lo, children are a heritage of the Lord;
and the fruit of the womb is His reward.

Psalm 127:3 KJV

Our sons may be as plants grown up in their youth;
Our daughters may be as cornerstones,
polished after the similitude of a palace.

Psalm 144:12 KJV

When the marriage chain first broke, your children seemed doomed. Surely this would destroy them! At the very least, they'd never lead normal lives. You could forget about carefree, happy childhood days for them. Theirs would be most unhappy and maladjusted.

The fears were intense and genuine. And in a way, your spouse shared them but was unable to compensate. You were frantic and appreciated any offer of help — even if it might fail. Things were desperate in those nothing-made-sense days. Humpty Dumpty had fallen off the wall and nothing could put him back together again.

If your children were not with you, you missed them terribly. You didn't know which was worse — not seeing them, or visiting them and then missing them all the more later. You were on a treadmill, and the ache was constant.

If you did have your children, they may have been the one thing that kept you going through the darkest days. No matter what their age, toddler or teen-ager, they needed you. You would have to be their rock of love. You may not have been capable of it yet. You may still have been in that numb stage. But if they and you were to make it, you would have to make it together . . . somehow.

> live
> in a perambulator
> and you never need walk . . .

You were frightened. Raising children was difficult enough within marriage — you didn't want the responsibility alone. You felt you couldn't cope with it, at least surely not at this time.

Even if time changed your reactions and fears regarding the children, some of the same concerns remain. If you have custody of the children, you're conscious of their many needs. There are the obvious physical ones, of course — food, clothing, shelter. These never posed the problem during your marriage that they do now. No matter how poor you were in the past, you are worse off now. Money — where will enough come from?

You must find a job. Or you must find a better job. There simply isn't enough money to pay the bills. While people can talk about child support being such a help, you know it will barely cover the baby-sitter's fee while you work. And who will you find to watch the children during the day? Who will give them the special love and care they need so badly now? Who can you trust? After a hard day at work, how will you be both the good father and mother to them? You simply don't know. But things will get better, you think — they will have to!

Now and then, just when everything seems on an even keel, a crisis arises. A child gets very ill, or falls off a porch, or swallows adult medication! You may need to rush the child to the hospital, but you have no way to get there. You look frantically for someone to take you, and you also need someone to baby-sit. When you eventually get to a doctor, you'll worry how you will pay the fee. And when you buy the prescriptions, you'll wonder how you'll balance the food budget later. But now your child is sick; that's all that matters! You feel ill, too, but so differently . . . .

> my little son
> is
> sick
>
> and so
> he
> sleeps
>
> how healthy
> his
>   illness
>   is

Much of your energy directed towards your children's needs goes towards their emotional and spiritual ones. They need to be loved — to be totally and completely immersed in love! God loves them — they must always be assured of that. And your love, no matter how great, will have to grow.

Children want their parents together; they want whole families, not fragmented ones. They'll do anything for this end. Older children may beg, scold, reprimand, and use logic. Younger ones may react with similar, yet immature, reasoning: "Let mommy get a new coat," for example, or "Don't feed daddy that awful green soup." Children want to know why — they want to know the truth. You will not be able to hedge their questions off forever, and it is better to be honest from the beginning. To deceive the children now will only hurt them more later. You'll level with them . . . and then level them with love.

But what explanations will help ease their loss? What rationalizations will compensate? Their questions may go on for years. Perhaps they'll never really understand — you sometimes wonder if you do yourself, completely. . . . Parents who desire divorce face the accusations of their children. Parents who grant divorce may also be accused. It is a terrifying thought. You've lost enough love, you don't want to lose your children's also.

have you ever killed something
        knowing it would not die?
but somewhere, in a life apart
it lives — and yet is dead.
and your children will ask you
        why you did it.
what will you answer? the truth?
        that it wanted to die . . .
will they believe you?

and the dead will live,
        separated . . .
and the living will live,
        separated . . .
never completely understanding
        the madness, the mess,
young and idealistic,
condemning the cheating,
you will not fulfill their lack
any more than they will understand your act.

teach them to swim
let no cramps strangle their emotions,
make them stronger
and then pray
they never need the strength,

that, somehow, beyond all logic,
they know as you,
that love existed in your loveless act.

Your children will be torn between love for you and love for their other parent. Their allegiance will be divided and may stay that way. You cannot expect anything different.

Your former mate and you have failed your children, and you will never make it up to them. Yet you must do everything you can to prove to your children that you are constant, to prove that you will not leave them, to prove that you will love them always.

You continue your day by day effort to show your affection. You know that material means will not assure it. What material proofs will comfort a child who cries through a nightmare or sits starry-eyed in a trance? What material proofs would ever compensate for a lost parent?

No, there are other, more effective ways to show love. You can take more time to pray and play with your youngsters. You can hold the little ones on your lap; you can rock them; you can read and sing to them. You can sit by the older ones as they watch TV, and you can put your arm around them or hold their hand as you talk together. You can pray together and discuss your faith and the constancy of our Lord who never leaves us and who never reneges on His love. You can worship together and make it an occasion of joy. You can share all types of indoor and outdoor activities with your children. And you can say, "I love you. I'm proud of you. I'm grateful God has given you to me."

The message should be repeated, one way or another, again and again. As you heal your children, you will be healed. They will help you through difficult hours. It is a two-way street, this street of love.

41

today you smiled
and your laughter
caught my heart.

today you smiled
and it was enough
if today you smile
tomorrow will i?

The peaceful, joyous side of your nature that you present
to your children may be more a brave front than reality. You
still need help. *You* still need to be comforted.

And all through the weeks and months you're working
to help "heal" your children, you wonder what is going
through the mind of the ex-mate. You wonder if the children
are remembered in that special way only a parent knows . . . .

do you hear
the cry in the night?

when all is still,
and the world in slumber,
are you awakened by the cry . . .
the personal, needful cry of your own?
does it reach past the miles
of city lights and night traffic
to where you lie, alone?

do you see as I, or
does the darkness protect you?
blotting out images?
can a cigarette calm you
distracting hands and heart?
will a drink nullify you
dulling old memories?

can a future cheer you,
          fulfilling all desires?
or will you always know?
will you always love?
will you always respond?
do you think
you will always hear
          the cry in the night?

that special cry,
          just for you . . . .

You don't know the answer. But *your* special cry is heard. You've cried it often enough to God. Surely He's heard it . . . hasn't He? When will He answer?
When?

How long wilt Thou forget me, O Lord?
     forever?
How long wilt Thou hide Thy face from me?
          Psalm 13:1 KJV

8 * Means of Coping

Thou hast seen, O Lord;
keep not silence.
O Lord, be not far from me.
Psalm 35:22 KJV

"How are you getting along?" your doctor asks.
"Just barely," you say. "Haven't you got something that
will help my temperament?"

You're over the hysteria and other extreme forms of
physical reactions now, but you still lack the stability of
your predivorce days. The period of depression has been replaced by a nervous, fidgety one. You try to control it most
of the time, but whenever the condition is combined with
weariness, problems, or setbacks of any kind, you find yourself snapping or even yelling at anyone nearby.

someone
took a rubber band,
knotted it in my
cranium
and then began to
twist . . .

beautifully
unfolding
in a blooming
blossom,
radiating the back

44

with taut
torture

someone
had unmitigated nerve,
to take my nerve
of crystal china,
and
chisel
and
chip

Stand BACK!

When I SCREAM,
the shrill
will
shatter,
the rubber band
will
reverberate,
the lymphs
will
limp.

You desperately yearn to relax. You're tired of the
backache, headache, stomachache, or any other physical
ache that characterizes the condition. You're tired of insomnia, yet this "tiredness" doesn't help put you to sleep.

Over the months you try or consider all the world's
standard remedies. If you smoked before, you double your
habit. The appeal of drinking to that "nonfeeling stage"
is great enough to even overcome an aversion for alcohol.
Perhaps drugs have become a temptation — at least the kind
doctors can prescribe. You're tempted to try all sorts of
means you'd never consider in better days, and you pray

for the strength to withstand such urges. You know that:

> No temptation has overtaken you that is not common
> to man. God is faithful, and He will not let you be
> tempted beyond your strength, but with the tempta-
> tion will also provide the way of escape that you may
> be able to endure it.
>
> *1 Corinthians 10:13 RSV*

You reflect on God's words and comfort. Like King Saul, you may let music — spiritual music — calm you during difficult periods. You worship, sing, pray, and read your Scriptures, but there are times when you almost think it's all a sham. Doubt flickers here and there, and you pray for more evidence of our Lord's reality and His love.

The Holy Spirit answers and strengthens you in many ways — one, through His people. God uses people to help people. He uses your pastor, your family, and your friends to help you . . . just as He will someday use you to help others.

There *are* Christians who take seriously our Lord's words:

> As the Father has loved Me, so have I loved you; abide
> in My love. . . . Love one another as I have loved you.
>
> *John 15:9, 12 RSV*

Or those of St. John:

> Let us love one another; for love is of God, and he
> who loves is born of God and knows God.
>
> *1 John 4:7 RSV*

The Spirit will provide at least one person who will be a friend — who will show you the Father's love through his or her love. This friend may not understand exactly what you're going through, but will *try* to understand and will be as close to emphathizing as any "outsider" can be. And you will value the friend greatly.

It is a rare experience
when one enjoys the unique friendship
that is ours . . .
A rapport that neither can explain,
as we cannot say
we always agree,
nor do we always perceive
the reality of each other's world.
Yet there is a depth
in each
the other cannot deny,
and there is an honesty
few would unmask.

I surely thank God
for this bond that lives
within the void
of both distance and time.
For if we saw the other not
and lived a hundred years
before again we met,
we would be friends
close still.
Because of that unique reality
that defies description,
That unexplainable existence
that escapes the mind's grasp,
That living appreciation
that I know
you know.
Of individual dancing
to a high frequency
we can both
hear.

Although all in the body of Christ with whom you worship Sunday after Sunday cannot be the one unique "friend" just mentioned, they can be a comfort just by their existence. Coming together to commune with God and His people can be the greatest joy you'll ever know. As you participate in the Eucharist, this joyous feast at the altar of God, you'll be assured that you have been forgiven, that you are loved, and that you will be strengthened. With the angels and archangels and, yes, all the company of saints in heaven and on earth, you will be praising God in peace and joy.

Praise ye the Lord.
Praise God in His sanctuary:
Praise Him in the firmament
of His power.
Let everything that hath breath
praise the Lord.
Praise ye the Lord.

Psalm 150:1, 6 KJV

9 * Ex-Mate

Then our mouth was filled with laughter,
And our tongue with shouts of joy.
Psalm 126:2 RSV

There is a bit of the romantic in everybody. We tend to think that life should have storybook endings. We begin our marriages with the assumption that marital problems will be minimal and we will live happily ever after. And even when we have been separated or divorced against our wishes, we believe that someday the nightmare will be over and the old love will bloom again.

If we were the party who wanted the divorce, it may have been because we thought we weren't appreciated. "She [or he] didn't understand me" is so common a complaint it has become a cliché. And if we didn't want the divorce, we felt the partner who did desire it certainly didn't appreciate us. If the other had only appreciated our love, we feel, things would have turned out differently. We really don't understand our ex-partner. How is it he or she missed this most obvious love of ours?

> i look at you
> and wonder
> why . . .
>
> i once knew you,
> i'm sure i
> did . . .

49

you were what i
wasn't,
and i knew
myself . . .
but now
who are you
anyway?
i was found
in loving
you,
while you were
lost
with love . . .

time is odd . . .
you can
give me explanations
tomorrow,
but make me happy

yesterday . . .

Yet because we did not succeed in marriage, our egos
are crushed — our self-esteem is low. In the back of our mind
is the suspicion — yes, fear — that we may not have what it
takes to remain married. We want to eventually prove ourselves in a second union, yet we dread the test — what if we
should fail again? We're no longer sure of ourselves or who
we are.

why analyze?
ACT!
though never a
gambler,
you dare not
avoid
fear

if once
and for all
is possible,
Jump!

FALL!
even,

but know
Who
is falling,
so that mirrors
mean
something

Meanwhile in this new setting — just behind us, yet still here — is the presence of our former marriage. Though it is dissolved, some ties remain. For one reason or another, we may come in contact with our former mate. And in discussing the visiting of the children, or the selling of the house, or the dividing of the joint property, or whatever, we find ourselves in an "almost married," "almost not married" situation.

We were divorced, amiably or angrily, yet there is still a "marriage" memory which only time can erase. There is even an attraction on occasion, and the meetings we have may very well develop into courting experiences, both consciously and unconsciously. Each partner may act more considerately to the other than they have in years. They may dress especially nice, for example, or prepare an excellent meal, or listen intently to a story they've heard dozens of times previously, forgetting for an interim all that passed between them in the near past.

The habit of a marriage — the years of living together — is very strong. But sooner or later, and usually sooner, the bubble bursts. Natural, negative characteristics of the partners, so irksome to each other, arise within a conversation or even within a somewhat romantic interlude. The rose-colored glasses break — the prince turns back into a frog, and Cinderella back into a scouring maid.

We feel very much like the guinea pigs and rats used in learning experiments — rats that are conditioned to pull levers for a reward. The day comes when the rewards cease, but the rats go on pulling the same levers anyway . . . to no avail. We wonder when we will finally learn that the ex-mate is no longer the answer for us. We know we learn most everything by experience. It seems *this* lesson will have to be learned more than once.

little rat
in the box,
how often
will you
pull?

how often
will they polish
the familiar lever
to make it
glow
promisingly . . .

little rat,
pensive and
still,
the lever looks
gold,
your paws turn
green

if learning is
learned

how long?
how
long?

There seems to be no stronger relationship than that of husband and wife, and the memories of a past union will never be completely erased. But although we will never be able to completely eradicate the experience because of its uniqueness, so also we will never again look to it for our help, for our comfort, for our life . . . no, not today . . . no, not in the many tomorrows to come . . . .

Now, however, we feel alone. We have nothing human to fill the empty place in our heart. And so we turn to our Creator for help.

I lift up my eyes to the hills.
From whence does my help come?
My help comes from the Lord,
Who made heaven and earth.
Psalm 121:1-2 RSV

It is God who will be a Refuge and our Strength. It is He who will sustain us. It may not seem that way now. It may seem little is sustaining us. The God of Abraham and Jacob . . . the God of Paul and Luther . . . our God . . . may seem a far way off. But hold on!

Wait on the Lord:
be of good courage,
and He shall strengthen
thy heart.
Wait,
I say,
on the Lord.

Psalm 27:14 KJV

53

10 * Dating

In Thee, O Lord, do I put my trust:
Let me never be put to confusion,
    Psalm 71:1 KJV

People look at you strangely nowdays. You don't feel any different, but others seem to think you are. If you are male, you are once again the unattached bachelor, and everyone assumes yours is a wild, wicked life. Husbands slap you on the back, wink, and ask how the "single" life is. Their wives suggest that you quit playing the field (even if you aren't) and think about settling down again.

If female, your very title has discriminatory connotations. You are labeled a *divorcee,* and everyone knows and apparently believes the cliché about divorcees. The conditions of your divorce make no difference; you are stuck with the degrading tag. Whatever your married moral scruples were, it is presumed you now have lost them, and sooner or later someone will drop a hint to that effect. Perhaps you'll even experience that unpleasant overture — the proposition of a married man who's the husband of a friend. There are always some who assume that all a divorcee needs is sexual satisfaction to make all her problems disappear. And it is always this same "brilliant" type who is "noble" enough to offer his services.

As for you, you want and need to begin a whole new social life. You turn to the church but may find you have no niche. Highest esteem is given to the married state (notwithstanding St. Paul's opinion), and many a couple feels you should date for one purpose only — to remarry. Nothing short of remarriage is honorable, whether you are ready for it or not.

Although the church is a proponent of marriage, it does little to help its single members change their status. Most congregational organizations are for one sex or the other (except the "couples" club, whose very name now offends you), and rarely is there an organization exclusively for single people of both sexes, outside of the young people's group.

You may have members in your congregation who introduce you to fellow Christians you find interesting. But if this does not happen, you will probably look elsewhere. You need companionship other than that of your unhappy memories, and you may turn to the secular world to find it. The reaction towards divorce there ranges from hostility to ambivalence. Yet on the surface most people project a "live and let live" attitude. People you meet are just "getting by" in life themselves. They have their own problems. They have no faith . . . they have no solutions . . . they cannot "help" you.

The church did not speak to your needs, seemingly, and neither do these newfound friends and acquaintances. But at first you may be very happy with their matter-of-factness towards your divorce. It is nice to be accepted as normal rather than as somewhat abnormal. And it's reassuring to find other people with insecurity problems. You had thought you were alone in this respect.

At secular gatherings you notice more and more of life's "cripples" — insecure people who so obviously need to blow their own horn that they make spectacles of themselves. You may even meet one whose ridiculous claims range from winning a war singlehandedly to mastering a language that doesn't exist.

> he really impressed me
> (course i'm easily impressed . . .)

> he had traveled the world
> and had mastered its speech.
> in France he spoke French,
> in Russia, of course Russian,
> Germany, German,
> Spain, Spanish,
> et cetera, et cetera . . .
> this exceptional linguist,
> this great man of letters,
> this worldwide traveler.

> but what made him unique,
> what impressed me no end,
> was the boast: "in Egypt
> i spoke Egyptian!"

> impressed without,
> laughing within,
> "Amazing!" said i
> as i watched him die . . .

> (but then i'm easily impressed,
> impressed easily am i . . . .)

Once you've entered these new circles, it isn't long before you begin to find people who are just like you — who are also divorced. You notice it seems more relaxing to talk to them than to most other people. An immediate rapport is common when two divorced people are introduced and left alone to converse. You find you can make a remark about your situation or past marriage and the other will respond with "I know exactly!" Once divorced, a person does know exactly . . . *exactly*.

And so the divorced form a new element — a world unto themselves. Once introduced, it will amaze you that outsiders are so unaware of it. This unique new world functions within the framework of the larger one, yet its members recognize each other and indicate the recognition right under the noses of the nonmembers. Indeed, as you meet more and more people in this new setting, you may begin to think of divorced friends and acquaintances as insiders, and of married, widowed, and other single people as outsiders.

The pull towards others like you can be very strong. It can be so strong, in fact, that you must recognize that it could pull you away from others like you in Christ — from the family of God. For it is this family, after all, that is the healthiest for you. It is within this family that you will experience the greatest comfort, peace, healing, and joy. It is the Spirit who guides and sustains you each day of your life. And unless He also governs the lives of your new friends, they will bring you no lasting happiness.

You will also meet widows and widowers among your new contacts. Nevertheless, although they also are without mates, you will have little in common with them and may find them less than satisfactory dates. Their allegiances are to the dead, while you have no such loyalty to your former spouse. And their memories of their marriages may be strong barriers to any new relationships you hope to build. You need to find yourself and to improve your self-esteem. You do not need someone who looks upon his or her married life as a success and upon yours as a failure.

But you *do* want to begin dating, and three out of four people do so within a year of their divorce. What you don't realize is that it's a whole new ball game out there. If you last dated back in the days when the big question was whether or not a kiss was appropriate for a first date, you're in for an eye-opener. No matter how sophisticated you think you may be . . . you aren't.

Dating is a game . . . and everybody's got his own set of rules. What is shocking or startling to the newly divorced Christian is the rules that are accepted as standard among formerly married men and women. A sexual pass is usual for first dates, and nine times out of ten it is an obvious and somewhat crude pass.

This conduct is not restricted to the male of the species, and often a newly divorced man will be shocked by the language and direct proposition of a woman who would have put the greatest Don Juan in his high school gang to shame. Females who are new to the "pass system" usually consider their date's proposal degrading. They may react to the "insult" with fear, or then again, with great rage! Many a date ends abruptly when the rules are not agreed upon.

Your biggest decision in any male-female relationship you enter is to clarify who you are, what your needs are, and how best you can fulfill your needs without compromising your nature as a child of God. This is a decision, and perhaps struggle, you must make with yourself and with your Lord. But it is one you cannot put off . . . because the rest of the world is not going to change.

Your happily married friends may be the first to give you advice and the last to understand your needs — theirs, after all, are taken care of. Some might even be shocked if you tried to explain that your divorce did not neutralize your gender. But you know it hasn't. And you know you are insecure. And you know you need love and acceptance. And you know you are subject to temptation. And you know better than to expect change in the "system."

for awhile
    i thought this one was different . . .
i, who have learned
    they are all the same.
i, who suspect,
    we are all the same . . .
imagine . . .
    just imagine . . .
if i won, obviously
    he lost.
all right, so i won.
    did i?
why can't i stay
    with one conclusion?
why do i sigh with relief
    and still want to kick myself?
why can't i always trust myself?
more important,
    why don't i always want to?

Bless you Naivete!
Bless you Righteous Conscience!
Bless you Contentment!
Bless you Stupidity!
Damn the Makers of 100 Assorted Flavors!
Damn the Market Appeal!
Damn the Distracting Distributors!
Damn the Curious Taste Buds!
Double Damn the Starving System!

For every Bathsheba there is a David . . . .

For every Joseph there is a Potiphar's wife . . . .

But your Bathsheba may never have married . . . .

And Potiphar's wife may now be divorced . . . .

59

Prepare to wrestle with the Angel of the Lord.
You will write the end of this chapter
afterwards . . . .

The Lord is nigh unto all them
  that call upon Him,
To all that call upon Him in truth.
He will fulfill the desire of them
  that fear Him;
He will also hear their cry
  and will save them.
The Lord preserveth all them
  that love Him.
  Psalm 145:18-20 KJV

11 * Extreme Doubt, Faith Challenged

I cry aloud to God . . . .
My soul refuses to be comforted.
I think of God, and I moan;
I meditate, and my spirit faints. . . .
I am so troubled that I cannot speak. . . .
Will the Lord spurn for ever,
*   and never again be favorable?*
Has His steadfast love forever ceased?
Are His promises at an end for all time?
Has God forgotten to be gracious?
Has He in anger shut up His compassion?
*   Psalm 77:1-4, 7-9 RSV*

Has God indeed forgotten you? Has He forgotten Himself? Who is He, anyway? And who are you?

Somewhere along the line you seem to have lost your identity. Now you're not really sure who you are. One personality is a ghostly shadow of the old you; one is a parent role; one is a professional image; one a social spirit; and so on. What it all adds up to is 1 and 1 and 1 and 1 and . . . and . . . and . . . but never a sum total. You've changed, you know, but you don't know *who* you've changed into . . . .

> what am i thinking about?
> i don't know, really

i just think . . .
everything runs together,
and yet there's no pattern.
not happy, not bitter,
i feel like an old woman
recalling memories,
some warm, some sad,
yet even the sadness is warm,
a poignant warmth,
a part of life.
it's as if i have
something to say,
something to tell,
and yet i can't tell
without destroying.
and anyway, you'd nod
but not know . . .

one begins to breathe
when oxygen is removed.
after the initial gasping,
choking and dying,
you lie so still
while life seeps slowly back
through each little pore.
and though you
again use a windpipe,
it is never enough.
some cell here
breathes one way,
another far off
wants something else.
each tiny cell,
small in itself,
yet a distraction

with memories,
a demand
of emotions.
each cell conflicting
yet each a part of you.

There is no quick grief period for divorce. The same
reactions, in varying degrees, occur again and again in the
months (and sometimes years) that follow. There is pain,
and dying, and flashes of freedom, and then again disap-
pointment. There is experimenting in new life styles, and
then depression when they fail to live up to hopes. There
is dormancy and apathy — colorless periods which cloud your
vision of God, yourself, and even a relationship between
you that is normally whole and vital.

i don't know, God
you seem so far . . .
it's me, i'm
sure
but somehow
you don't seem
real

are you only here
when i need you?
even i know
better

i've been existing so long
without you
really
oh, i talk of you
but not really
to you

i think my soul is dressed
in gray
no, not even gray
just sort of
nothing . . .
somewhere it lost
its brightly colored
frock

when you find it
will you bring it back
to me?
i think if i had it
i'd see you again

i think if i had it
i'd know where
i am

Perhaps your uncertainty and self-doubts stem from the old questions which have never been answered: Why? What failed? Was it I? Should I have? Should I have not? What good will come from it? Why did it happen?

During the darker hours of periods like this you have no idea that the future holds brighter days. They can be right around the corner, but they may as well be a planet away. You cannot see the dim dusk of tomorrow, let alone the bright sunshine of a month or year away. You know only suspicion, and doubt, and uncertainty, and a fear of new beginnings. God has humbled you. There are periods of introspection which leave you stripped of any dignity and of all merit. You've recognized the innermost parts of your being and have confessed with Paul, "I am the foremost of sinners." (1 Timothy 1:15 RSV)

You have been wounded; you have been bitter; you have been in pain; but you have never yet cursed your Maker.

Always you have clung to the reality of God's love; even when you wanted to escape it, it followed you as the "hound of heaven." You could not shake off your faith. You could not run from your God. No, if you fled to the heavens, He was at the top; if you peered into chasms, He was at the bottom. However dim your flame of faith, you could not snuff it out. You clung to that tiny match barely glowing in the blizzard around you. It was the eye of the tornado — the source of perfect peace. Even when you didn't realize it, it was the staple that stapled you.

If anyone were to have told you that you'd ever give up on God, you would have responded as Peter did — perhaps others, but never you. Still, you have doubts that mount daily; there are, in fact, times when you reflect on your naiveté in ever believing that belief itself would be a cure-all, or that the Scriptures could be words of comfort rather than meaningless syllables not backed by love in evidence. Nevertheless, to give up on God? To deny His validity? To question His promise?

Yet it's possible. You may do all this . . . and more . . . . If you are disappointed once too often, if you have one too many straws placed on your back, if you wear out before rest refreshes — well, then, you may just lose your Job patience. You may have "had it" with life. You may spill out pent-up emotions in an uncontrolled attack on God Himself. You may begin a prayer, turn it into a curse, and end it in defeat. You will be shocked by your audacity. But like a dam burst, nothing will stop you until the winds of the hurricane have exhausted themselves.

> Dear God,
>   Help Me!
> You're the only one who cares . . .
> the only one who's true . . .
> the only one i can trust . . .

What a fool i was,
what a fool i am,
Day by day i see
how weak, how naive
        i am.
How much humbling do i need?
God, help me!

God, don't try me anymore.
I am prostrate.
I give in.
I can't bear more.
If we are playing a game,
I concede.
End it.
I can't go on.
God, I who need forgiveness
can't forgive you.

Have you no pity?
no love at all?
Do you laugh too?
are you the devil disguised?
Forgive me, but
i am sick of your trials,
sick to death of your tests,
i never pass, anyway.
Just leave me alone!

Don't you Dare
        use me as Job . . .
Find another!
i refuse to be your example!
if this is what you are,
if this is what you expect,
if this is what you demand,

> i renounce you!
> i am sorry i ever heard of you!
> i regret the day i turned to you
> because you refused to help!
>> I must help myself,
>> what need of you?
>
> God, why?
> forgive me my failings.
> i want to believe,
> but even You
> have failed me.

You should be terrified at your words . . . but your faith is not that awake. You have given up on God; You feel He has deserted you like all the rest. You hope it will not last — this doubt — but you do not know.

Right now it is too real to believe it will ever be otherwise.

> The night racks my bones,
> and the pain that gnaws me takes no rest. . . .
> God has cast me into the mire,
> and I have become like dust and ashes.
> I cry to Thee and Thou dost not answer me;
> I stand, and Thou dost not heed me.
> Thou hast turned cruel to me;
> with the might of Thy hand Thou dost persecute me.
>> *Job 30:17, 19-21 RSV*

Perhaps for the first time in your life you know what total desertion is. . . . Perhaps for the first time in your life you know what hell must be. . . . Perhaps for the first time in your life you understand the enigma of our Lord's cry from the cross:

Eloi, Eloi, lama sabachthani? . . .
My God, my God, why hast Thou forsaken Me?

Mark 15:34 RSV

The Lord is silent. He does not speak. He does not hear.
He must not care.

Perhaps for the first time in your life the Psalms *really*
become yours. . . .

My God, my God, why hast Thou forsaken me?
Why art Thou so far from helping me,
    and from the words of my groaning?
O my God, I cry by day
    but Thou dost not answer;
And by night,
    but find no rest.

Psalm 22:1-2 RSV

12 * Recovery from Doubt, Faith Rebuilt

The fool hath said in his heart,
   "There is no God."
   Psalm 53:1 KJV

For an hour, a day, a month, perhaps years, you may doubt. You may believe God, if there is a God, has cast you aside — has forgotten you. You may ignore Him completely or bewail your fate and cry as did Job:

Let the day perish wherein I was born. . . .
Why did I not die at birth,
   come forth from the womb and expire? . . .
I have no rest; but trouble comes. . . .
The night is long, and I am full of tossing
   till the dawn. . . .
Lo, He passes by me, and I see Him not;
   He moves on, but I do not perceive Him.
   Job 3:3, 11, 26; 7:4; 9:11 RSV

You don't believe. And "unless you see signs and wonders you will not believe" (John 4:48 RSV). The present is so overwhelmingly real, you cannot see into the future. But it's there. And God has a plan for you in it. "God is greater than man" (Job 33:12 RSV). And He can take greatest evil that happens to you and bring good out of it.

For "we know that in everything God works for good with those who love Him." (Romans 8:28 RSV)

There is a reason God chastens you . . . or allows you to be chastened. God gives you a new chance for a new life. He silently observes your moods of doubt and self-pity; He patiently listens to your endless complaints; but then He finally roars back, *Just who do you think you are to question Me?*

> Where were you
> > when I laid the foundations of the earth? . . .
> Is it by your wisdom that the hawk soars
> > and spreads his wings toward the south?
> Is it at your command that the eagle mounts up
> > and makes his nest on high? . . .
> Shall a faultfinder contend with the Almighty?
> He who argues with God, let him answer it.
> > *Job 38:4; 39:26-27; 40:2 RSV*

But you have no answers . . . . You still don't understand God, though you begin to believe enough to be frightened. Your faith starts to thaw out and you marvel at your previous audacity. Yet, for all of your unfaithfulness, you hear the Almighty telling you to relax and put your trust in Him. He assures you that "all things are possible to him who believes" (Mark 9:23 RSV). Your answer is a cry, "[Lord], I believe; help my unbelief!" (Mark 9:24 RSV.) You cling to the hope that God *has* control . . . that God *does* care . . . and that God *can* change your life. . . .

> Behold, God does all these things
> > twice, three times with a man,
> To bring back his soul from the Pit,
> > that he may see the light of life.
> > *Job 33:29 RSV*

You begin to realize that what happened to you was not God's will, for the God who is love wills only good for His loved ones. You know that your quarrel is not with God, that you are contending not "against flesh and blood, but against the principalities, against the powers, against the world rulers of this present darkness, against the spiritual hosts of wickedness in the heavenly places" (Ephesians 6:12 RSV). And you say to God, "You can't let me fight this alone. I need more help. I need You!"

You remind God of His covenant with you. Luther said when we are oppressed by sin or conscience we must retort, "But I am baptized! And if I am baptized, I have the promise that I shall be saved, and have eternal life, both in soul and body!"

So you remind God of your baptism and of His promise of love. You hold Him to it. You hang on even if He doesn't seem to notice you. You are one of His children, and even if you weren't, you could demand at least "the crumbs that fall from their master's table" (Matthew 15:27 RSV). You "wait on the Lord" (Psalm 27:14 KJV), but you don't give up. And He *does* come. If you ask Him, He does come ... perhaps "in a dream, in a vision of the night" (Job 33:15 RSV), perhaps in a rush of the Spirit, perhaps in a quiet rebuilding of confidence and faith in Him. But He *will come* . . . because *He is*. . . .

In the name of the
Father
Son
and
Holy Ghost

Amen

Dear Lord,

Dear Friend,

i've stopped walking
          to think
and crying
          to pray
and fighting
          to submit

and You are right . . .
Jacob wrestled an angel.
          did i
          unknowing?

i am exhausted
          weak
Raggedy Ann,
straw strewn on the floor,

my head drops,
my senses sag,
and i would sleep
          would sleep
          would sleep
through roaring scores
of Catskill pins

Glorious Lord,
to give one
this composing point
when frame no longer
          can resist,
and mind, encased,
          must rest.

i thank You, God
for strength that surrounds

and seeps within,
till i would rise and shout
    "God's here!
    right here!
    He stays
and sustains
and secures
    ME!"

As a rug whipped
i am dustless.
If anyone walks,
my fibers stand firm.

Just a short while ago you had a shaken faith . . . and
no hope. You were as good as dead.

    My spirit is broken, my days are extinct,
        the grave is ready for me. . . .
    Where then is my hope?
    Job 17:1. 15 RSV

But now all has changed. Now the prayer of your loved
ones has been answered: "May the God of hope fill you with
all joy and peace in believing so that by the power of the
Holy Spirit you may abound in hope" (Romans 15:13 RSV).
Now you know:

    There is a Holy Spirit!
        As real as sodium chloride
        on the cheek . . .
        Yes, more so . . .
    And there is sin,
        yes, and so personal
        too personal . . .
        too narcistic. . . .

I have to get away
to see the mirror
And it's a shock —
the impatience
I see,
and the sin
of self-love
and will
But it's a joy —
God's love and peace
Because they erase the image,
and the Holy Spirit
gives hope
and help!
And tears of remorse
are as a
baptism . . .

God has seen you through this . . . in spite of yourself.
He will see you through the future . . . in spite of yourself.
God loves you . . . in spite of yourself.

I waited patiently for the Lord; and He
inclined unto me and heard my cry.
He brought me up also out of a horrible pit,
out of miry clay,
and set my feet upon a rock,
and established my goings.
And He hath put a new song in my mouth,
even praise unto our God.
Psalm 40:1-3 KJV

13 * Ready to Begin Anew

O Lord, Thou hast searched me and known me!
Thou knowest when I sit down and when I rise up;
Thou discernest my thoughts from afar.
Thou searchest out my path and my lying down,
and art acquainted with all my ways.
Even before a word is on my tongue,
lo, O Lord, Thou knowest it altogether.
Thou dost beset me behind and before,
and layest Thy hand upon me.
Such knowledge is too wonderful for me;
it is high, I cannot attain it.

Psalm 139:1-6 RSV

God knows you far better than you know your-self. He has been with you through it all—He knew how you'd feel and react before you did. And He knew you would change. He knew the day would come when you would stop rereading Volume One of your life and would begin exploring Volume Two.

And it would be a day of freedom—a day of victorious elation. If your heart flipped long ago when you first felt love for your mate, it now will burst with joy as that love flees. It's like an iron cage opened—you're no longer a prisoner to it—the "new you" can step out. You may have been separated or divorced before, but *now* you are free. There is no emotion left . . . and you are anxious to begin a new life.

no emotion . . .

> save the urgency to be done!
> to have it finished!
> to be free!
> to meet the adventures of life.
> to start anew,
>> having learned.
> to enjoy all.
> to take each gift
>> and savor its pecularity.
> to grab the future!
> to take each minute,
>> and make all meaningful.
> to give myself!
> to ask for nothing,
>> and find everything
>> in nothing.
> to seek God's plan!
> to find myself,
> to be myself!
> to use my gifts,
> to drain my resources.
> to flee to life!
>> to grasp it gratefully,
>> to sing its praises,
>> to laud its blessings.

no emotion . . . save urgency!

One of the first things you must do to begin the new life is to get a new image of yourself. You've lived with a sense of failure far too long — it's time to discard it! If you are a woman, society has by and large measured your success by how well you've pleased your husband. A wife is usually stereotyped in a role that discounts her as an individual . . . as a person . . . and if the husband no longer wants her, she immediately supposes she has failed as a woman and something is intrinsically wrong. If you are a male, this is probably not the way you feel, but there are many ways failure can be tagged, and you may be suffering from another variety that is just as unjust and frustrating.

Either way, you must begin looking at yourself with new hope . . . no, not just with hope, but with new confidence. The process of healing puts the odds in favor of a new, fulfilling life. But *you* can't stand in the way. *You* can't put up obstacles that prevent new growth — obstacles as clinging to the past with its hurts and disappointments, as seeking revenge for supposed wrongs, as giving up or lacking zest for new ventures.

It is true that you had to work out your grief slowly . . . with tears and talk and time. But that is ninety-nine percent over now and you are ready to begin anew. Now you can look in the mirror and see someone you like, not dislike. Now you can have the courage to go out and do something you've always wanted to do, but were afraid to try. Now you can experience a rejuvenating intoxication with life and with yourself that will make you more self-assured than you've ever been. There can be times when you feel so self-confident that you'd like to talk with kings and entertain queens. The whole world is a challenge and few feats feared.

And this new you, as it blossoms and develops, will attract others. If the new strength is not built on vanity or lovelessness, people will enjoy your company. You will again be a person worth liking . . . and if you're fortunate, worth loving. . . .

> The joy of being loved!
>> is there anything greater?
> To love
>> and know it brings response.

To know the security
>that it will endure through
>the impossible,
>and is yours to accept fully
>if all else fails.
A love that's free,
>that exists no matter
>what your choice.
That respects your confusion,
>and self-doubt,
>and responsibilities.
That can live without
>immediate fulfillment.
That says — you are free,
>do as you must . . .
>>I am here.

Whether you have new love or not, you can become anything you want to become. You can come out of this in better shape than you went into it — stronger, more poised, more confident of yourself than ever. You can do it, but you have to make the effort. You can't just sit back and do nothing. You must *ask* for the change. It will be given to you. (Matthew 7:7)

And you must begin *working* for the change. In order to make a new beginning, you must first of all understand yourself . . . you must have insight into what makes you tick.

One way to find out is to keep a notebook of yourself, or really of your reactions to everyday happenings. If something bothers you during the day, write down what it is. Then write down where it happened, what you were doing at the time, how you felt just before it happened, and any other such detail. Make a note of how your feelings were hurt, or what frustrated you, or what pressured you, and the like. Note also who the party or parties involved were. Follow the same procedure with happy incidents each day. Record not merely each joyous incident, but what happened before and after it.

After a month or so, read your "account book." You'll be surprised to find a pattern — a list of conditions, activities, and people who are good and bad medicine for you. Then use this insight to embrace what is good for you and to avoid what is bad.

Remember that this is your life, not someone else's. Don't let others make you over into their images. Don't let others decide what is right for you on the basis of what is right for them. If you remarry someday, still stay yourself. Never become a mere reflection of your new mate, unless this is what the real you wants.

If you do not feel ready for marriage, don't rush into it. Instead live through this period of new beginnings without making a commitment. Be sure of yourself; enjoy your life now before you put it in a new setting. There will always be a tomorrow; do not push it before you are ready. But do not close your mind to it. . . . There may be something even better in your future.

listen
to your bells now
pealing
       carefree color
ringing
       sweeping freedom
the great golden
bells

listen to them now
the sound travels

and is
gone

time effaces
the enchanting melody
of even an
echo

someday
you'll stand
right under the bells
looking up at a
tarnished
trim

then
when your bells
have a
haunting hollow
ring

      consider
my
warm wedding
ring

You don't know what the future will bring. It may be
that the present which you find so interesting today will pale
tomorrow. You may wish to enjoy it for still a while. Yet
you wonder . . . perhaps God has already opened tomorrow's
door for you.

yesterday
i was following a Falcon
on Lake Shore Drive,
and as my car
sweeped and swooped,

i remembered
the swift sweet
skylarks. . . .

today,
in an alley,
i passed a school door
and heard a bell,
again i remembered. . . .

tomorrow
perhaps i'll see
a heavy black coat,
or hear the Psalms
chanted,
or smell
red red roses,
or taste dry
white wine,
and i'll remember. . . .

i'll remember. . . .

Your future's up to you . . . and yet not you alone. Don't try to change yourself without God's help. Don't begin a new life that doesn't center on Him. Ask yourself what alternatives there are for lifelong fulfillment and satisfaction. Look at the neighbor next door, the worker at the next desk. Ask if the endless cleaning, for example, or double workweeks work. Check if meaningless chatter or continual kaffee klatsches console. See if the extended social life or daily drinking bring any lasting bubbles. Question whether dabbling in the occult or embracing astrology result in any reliable answers or inner peace. Inspect all the alternatives you can and then compare them to the One who says:

"Peace I leave with you; My peace I give to you; not as the world gives do I give to you." (John 14:27 RSV)

If you have slipped and fallen, get up and walk back. Change *with* your Lord, not without Him. For it is He who came that all "may have life, and have it abundantly" (John 10:10 RSV). And the abundant life isn't just a "You and me, God" proposition. It isn't something you meditate about now and then as you ride a commuter train or work in your garden. It's being alive and active within His people or staying dead and dormant without. The blessings you reap will be in ratio to the interest you sow. So find the congregation that is most like "home" for you. Make it your family in Christ, eat at its table, and rejoice in its home. For "if anyone is in Christ, he is a new creation." (2 Corinthains 5:17 RSV)

What shall I render to the Lord
    for all His bounty to me?
I will lift up the cup of salvation
    and call on the name of the Lord,
I will pay my vows to the Lord
    in the presence of all His people. . . .
Praise the Lord!

Psalm 116:12-14, 19 RSV

14 * New Life — and Love

Verily God hath heard me;
He hath attended to the voice of my prayer.
Blessed be God, who hath not turned away
    my prayer, nor His mercy from me.
    Psalm 66:19-20 KJV

Therefore my heart is glad, and my glory
    rejoiceth; my flesh also shall rest in hope.
Thou wilt shew me the path of life;
    in Thy presence is fullness of joy,
at Thy right hand there are pleasures
    forevermore.
    Psalm 16:9, 11 KJV

In many ways life seems its old self again. Your children, yelling from your window to a neighbor's, sound very much like children all over the world. Their singsongy, calling voices remind you of yours as a child.

> hey Scaaa
> deee . . .
>
> canya come owww
> ttt?
> ask your maaa
> ther!
>
> Nooo, let's play
> herrre . . .

83

i donwanna . . .
come over myyy
house . . .

no, i
won't

i donlikeyu
either!

comaww
nnn . . .

pleezzz . . .

Everybody says you're the way you used to be. You know you're not. You know you will never be the same person again. You've lived too much. You've changed. But you know what your friends mean. You're healthy and whole, and the future can only get better. You'll always respect the experience you had. It was hell . . . and yet a cleansing by fire. It was a humbling healing and has made you more aware and understanding of others' problems and weaknesses.

The period has passed when your means of coping were extreme — totally immersing yourself in your work or in your children or in your leisure life. When you turn to new activities now, it is not because they are means of escape, but because you enjoy them and they express the new you. Now you're really getting something out of those evening classes you attend; cooking is once more a joy; tennis has become a refreshing sport; and your social activities are now a matter of choice rather than need.

You're even thinking of remarriage again. Oh, maybe not yet, but at least you no longer say you'll *never* remarry! You're surprised at the lack of understanding some close friends and relatives have when you indicate you may cast off your somber mourning cloak and trade it in for a coat of many colors. The possibilities before you in life are numerous, and you are now ready to start investigating them.

> for two years
> i walked a tightrope . . .
> a long slender rope
> that led nowhere . . .
>
> and nowhere was still . . .
> and endless . . .
> and the rope, slack.
>
> Everyone smiled
> and scattered nets
> yelling bravo!
>
> and now
> it's a rope
> tight
> with short jets
> to the
> EVERYWHERE
> near!

For some time your youngest children have been asking each new date, "Are you going to be my new daddy [or mommy]?" It has proven embarrassing at times and humorous at others. But the youngsters mean it. It is not uncommon for children to *want* two parents in a home. They may even tell you to go out and find a husband or wife. Older children may have more reservations, and of course there are some youngsters who are just out-and-out against the whole idea. But children who feel loved by you will not be threatened. They know something is missing in their home, and they want life as perfect as possible.

There are various reasons why you may consider giving up even a fascinating, richly blessed single life to reenter the state of matrimony. You may miss the home life you once knew—the sounds of children about the house, the smells of the kitchen, the warmth of a "filled" dwelling rather than an empty, lonely apartment. You may miss the day-by-day companionship of someone who really cares and is truly interested in even the little things that make up your world. You may miss having someone to share the children's accomplishments and to help you in raising them. You may wish to give your children a "complete" home with two live-in parents. You may miss the sexual fulfillment and joy that can be found in a good marriage. You may wish to resume the role of husband or wife which you truly loved.

You may have many a reason . . . or none. Yes, even none. . . . For even if you are hesitant about another lifelong commitment, you may be blessed with a love that is worthy of no less.

one night
    i looked and knew . . .
nothing was said,
but i knew then
    as never before.

odd, how calm
    our eyes were.
not a thought lay covered,
an emotion concealed,
    all was shared . . .
my mind was racing
    to tell you,
my heart begged to cry out . . .
but as each word
fluttered there on my lips . . .
your eyes glowed their reflection.

one night
    i looked and knew . . .

that you knew, too.

Love is still the major reason for remarrying. And
divorced people by and large are marrying people. It is possible to learn from one's mistakes and to make a second
marriage a much happier one than the first — in fact, one
that can in no way be compared to the first.

Even if you had few complaints regarding your former
union, you may find that the new marriage is a brilliant
gem — as different from the old as champagne is from beer.
The beer may have gone flat, but the champagne bubbles
can last *if* . . . *if* you do not marry the same type of person
you did before (though there are some exceptions to this
"if"); *if* you know who you are and can evaluate your
strengths and faults realistically; *if* you and your new mate
make God the most important part of your lives; *if* you keep
the lines of communication open between you always; *if*
you continue to respect each other as individual persons
rather than role-players of your own making; *if* you keep
faithful to each other while faithful to yourselves.

free   free   free

independently
free
and yet one
with you. . . .

what a phenomenon!
i'm me,
and you and me,
and part of you,
and yet me.

see how love
does
freely bind:
a mysterious
one but two,
or is it
two but one?
until two are,
they can never know
the blessed state.
little wonder
God can be Triune. . . .

It is a common fallacy, however, to judge a divorced person's rehabilitation in terms of whether he or she has successfully remarried. Marriage is not for everyone, nor should all people be expected to fulfill themselves in the same way. Many a divorced person feels that remaining single is not as dreadful as society — married society, that is — would have them believe. They know it is possible for a person to lead a joyous, fulfilling life as *either* a single or married person.

The God who is love gives us love in many, many ways. He offers us all gifts if we but open our hearts and accept them. He tells us to look around and see all the manifestations of His blessings.

Life *can* be beautiful! It *can* be a thing of beauty — a joy forever. There are so many blessings available in life that we cannot comprehend them all. And there is no way we can fully appreciate God or the gifts He has in store for us.

O the depth of the riches and wisdom
and knowledge of God!
How unsearchable are His judgments
and how inscrutable His ways!

"For who has known the mind of the Lord,
    or who has been His counselor?"

"Or who has given a gift to Him
    that he might be repaid?"

For from Him and through Him and
    to Him are all things.
To Him be glory forever. Amen.

Romans 11:33-36 RSV

To Him be all glory. It is He who has given us physical life and has upheld us when it was weak! It is He who has sent His Son to save us from eternal death! It is He who has sent His Spirit to fill us with new life! God is the Alpha and the Omega — the beginning and the end of love and life. We can only respond to Him and to His unmerited gifts with the shout of the psalmist!

Bless the Lord, O my soul;
    and all that is within me,
    bless His holy name!
Bless the Lord, O my soul,
    and forget not all His benefits,
who forgives all your iniquity,
    who heals all your diseases,
who redeems your life from the Pit.
    who crowns you with steadfast
    love and mercy,
who satisfies you with good
    as long as you live
    so that your youth is
    renewed like the eagle's. . . .
Bless the Lord, O my soul!

Psalm 103:1-5, 22 RSV

Postscript

Even in the lives of Christians,
most certainly in the lives of Christians . . .

There can be times when all reason and logic vanish,
When Evil envelopes our lives,
When all is madness, or suffering, or emptiness,
        or despair,
When not only the box bottom breaks,
        but the side supports collapse,
When *what could never happen in our family does,*
When despairing depths of doom loom in the darkness,
And fish on shore flop frantically to find the familiar,
When pain persists . . . pounding, pounding . . .
And cancer cuts through every cell,
When all the persistent planning, training, and loving
        of a lifetime
        smashes and shrivels into shattered junk. . . .

Even in the lives of Christians,
most certainly in the lives of Christians . . .

There are times when the pastor no longer can play
        the physician,
When family and friends can no longer heal,
When the patient can no longer digest oral pills
        and comforting couplets,
When faith has reached the fray of the rope,
        and sackcloth is no balm to the boil,
When no human can help . . . and God seems love-dry,

When one repeats like a ruined record, "Why, Why,
          Just tell me why!"
And the answer is silence . . . sustained, still . . .
When God has walked away, as if in Gethsemane,
And one realizes for the first time
The hope less-ness-ness of Christ's screammm . . .
          "My God, My God, Why Hast Thou
          Forsaken Me?"

Even in the lives of Christians,
most certainly in the lives of Christians . . .

From far in the distance, from where God has walked,
          comes rumbling thunder . . . resounding, sounding . . .
"BE STILL AND KNOW THAT I AM GOD!
You Question My Love? I AM Love!"

And silence reigns and silence sustains

And then if one hears . . . through one's tears,
And then if one's still . . . and works His will,
And then if one stays . . . to await His ways.

Then one WILL know,
          will know God's love,
          and receive His Spirit,
          and, perhaps, finally

                    see

                         why. . . .

I give thee Thanks, O Lord,
*   with my whole heart. . . .*
Though I walk in the midst
*   of trouble,*
Thou dost preserve my life . . . .

The Lord will fulfill
His purpose for me.
Thy steadfast love, O Lord,
endures forever.
Psalm 138:1, 7-8 RSV